Unlocking the Secrets of Science

Profiling 20th Century Achievers in Science, Medicine, and Technology

William Hewlett: Pioneer of the Computer Age

•••

Kathleen Tracy

Mitchell Lane
PUBLISHERS

PO Box 196 • Hockessin, Delaware 19707
www.mitchelllane.com

Unlocking the Secrets of Science

Profiling 20th Century Achievers in Science, Medicine, and Technology

William Hewlett: Pioneer of the Computer Age

....

Copyright © 2003 by Mitchell Lane Publishers, Inc. All rights reserved. No part of this book may be reproduced without written permission from the publisher. Printed and bound in the United States of America.

Printing   2   3   4   5   6   7   8   9   10

Library of Congress Cataloging-in-Publication Data
Tracy, Kathleen.
     William Hewlett: pioneer of the computer age/ Kathleen Tracy.
       p. cm — (Unlocking the secrets of science)
     Summary: Profiles William Hewlett, co-founder of the Hewlett Packard Company, which has been producing electronics equipment since 1939.
     Includes bibliographical references and index.
     ISBN 1-58415-142-0
     1. Hewlett, William R. —Juvenile literature. 2. Electronics engineers—United States—Biography—Juvenile literature. 3. Hewlett-Packard Company—History—Juvenile literature. 4. Business-people—United States—Biography—Juvenile literature. [1. Hewlett, William R. 2. Engineers. 3. Inventors. 4. Scientists. 5. Hewlett-Packard Company—History. 6. Businesspeople.] I. Title. II. Series.
TK140.H48T73 2002
621.381'092—dc21
[B]   2002011058

ABOUT THE AUTHOR: Kathleen Tracy has been a journalist for over twenty years. Her writing has been featured in magazines including The Toronto Star's "Star Week," *A&E Biography* magazine, *KidScreen* and *TV Times*. She is also the author of numerous biographies including "The Boy Who Would Be King" (Dutton), "Jerry Seinfeld - The Entire Domain" (Carol Publishing) and "Don Imus - America's Cowboy" (Carroll & Graf). She recently completed "God's Will?" for Sourcebooks.

CHILDREN'S SCIENCE REVIEW EDITOR: Stephanie Kondrchek, B.S. Microbiology, University of Maryland

PHOTO CREDITS: cover: AP Photo; pp. 6, 8 AP Photo; pp. 10, 11, 12 Corbis; p. 18 Hewlett-Packard; pp. 20, 24 AP Photo; p. 26 Corbis; p. 29 Hewlett-Packard; p. 30 AP Photo; p. 31 Corbis; p. 32 AP Photo; pp. 36, 37 Hewlett-Packard; p. 38 Al Luckow; p. 42 Hewlett-Packard

PUBLISHER'S NOTE: In selecting those persons to be profiled in this series, we first attempted to identify the most notable accomplishments of the 20th century in science, medicine, and technology. When we were done, we noted a serious deficiency in the inclusion of women. For the greater part of the 20th century science, medicine, and technology were male-dominated fields. In many cases, the contributions of women went unrecognized. Women have tried for years to be included in these areas, and in many cases, women worked side by side with men who took credit for their ideas and discoveries. Even as we move forward into the 21st century, we find women still sadly underrepresented. It is not an oversight, therefore, that we profiled mostly male achievers. Information simply does not exist to include a fair selection of women.

Contents

William Hewlett has always been characterized as an affable engineer. He co-founded electronics giant Hewlett-Packard Company with his friend, David Packard. He was a Silicon Valley pioneer as he helped guide the company he co-founded into the computer age.

Chapter 1
An Electronic Supernova

• •

Silicon Valley, which is home to the largest concentration of technical firms in the world, gets its name from the element used to make the basic components of the computer and other electronics. Most people associate Silicon Valley with people like Bill Gates and Steven Jobs who spearheaded the personal computer boom of the 1980s and 1990s. But the foundation of Silicon Valley was actually laid at the *beginning* of the last century with the work of Lee de Forest.

De Forest was born in Council Bluffs, Iowa, in 1873, and as a child was fascinated with machinery. By the time he was 13 he had started inventing his own gadgets such as a miniature blast furnace. For a while, he put aside his interest in science because it was his father's wish that he study to be a minister. But eventually de Forest followed his heart instead and continued pursuing his inventions.

While in school, he was constantly tinkering, hoping to invent something he might be able to sell or enter in a contest. De Forest was a bit obsessed with the idea of becoming famous, but early on, none of his inventions were successful.

Lee earned his Ph.D. from Yale in 1896 with a dissertation, which is a long research paper, on radio waves. A few years later he developed an improved wireless telegraph receiver, which led him to found the De Forest Wireless Telegraph Company in 1902. But as would be the case repeatedly throughout his life, the company failed because de Forest was not a smart businessman.

Lee de Forest (right), inventor of the audion tube, which preceded the transistor in communications electronics, presents one of his original tubes to Reginald Hawkins, chief of the Science and Technology Division of the New York Public Library, April 8, 1952. William Hewlett was inspired by de Forest's work and life.

Lee doggedly pursued his inventions and became among the first in the United States to work in what would become known as radio. And his work with vacuum tubes, devices that contain a number of electrodes inside a tube with virtually no air in it, would be de Forest's greatest achievement.

In 1907 he patented a device he called the Audion, which was a special kind of vacuum tube that was able to amplify weak electric signals, meaning it was able to "hear" wireless signals better than previous vacuum tubes. In 1910 he moved to California and got a job at the Federal Telegraph Company in Palo Alto. Palo Alto is located in a valley that is 50 miles long and extends between San Francisco and San Jose. Back then, it was called Valley of Heart's Delight, primarily because of its abundance of orchard crops, such as apricots. In addition to being famous for its fruit tress, the valley was home to the world-famous Stanford University, which helped pay for some of de Forest's research.

The Audion had many possible uses, including detecting radio signals and amplifying sound. It could also transmit speech and music. In 1912 Lee and two coworkers at Federal Telegraph Company used the Audion to listen to a fly's footsteps as it walked across paper. The Audion worked so well, de Forest would later say it sounded as if the fly were wearing marching boots. This event was the first time that a vacuum tube had been used to amplify a signal.

De Forest sold the Audion to the telephone company for $50,000—a huge amount of money at the time. The telephone company planned to use it to amplify transcontinental wired phone calls. De Forest continued to make improvements in the Audion. In 1916 he was able to use it as an oscillator, a device that generates radio or audio frequencies, during a series of experimental broadcasts he presented from Columbia Phonograph Laboratories. De Forest had shown that with this one device, you could transmit, receive and amplify radio signals, marking the birth of electronics. It would eventually be the foundation for the development of radio, television, radar, tape recorders and even computers.

Steve Jobs co-founded Apple Computer Company, and was partially responsible for the personal computer boom that took place in the 1980s and 1990s. His technical partner, Steve Wozniak, had worked for Hewlett-Packard in the 1970s, but left in 1976 to join Jobs, when Hewlett-Packard did not choose to expand into personal computers at that time.

And from this single invention, an entire new technological industry would eventually evolve and settle in Palo Alto and the rest of Silicon Valley. Over half of the 100 largest electronics and software companies in the world started in Silicon Valley, including Hewlett-Packard, which began as the dream of two young college students, William Hewlett and his best friend, Dave Packard.

Hewlett is quick to acknowledge the importance of de Forest's legacy, comparing the scientist to a supernova, a star that after exploding continues to remain visible for years. Often, the supernova is so bright that it obscures entire galaxies. According to Hewlett, de Forest's work caused a technological ripple effect that set the stage for many of the 20th century's most important electronic inventions. Hewlett himself was inspired by the inventor, but as a boy he never dreamed that one day he would not only invent a product that would prove just as enduring as the Audion, but be credited for being one of the founders of Silicon Valley.

Bill Gates is the co-founder of Microsoft. He and partner Paul Allen were originally hired by Ed Roberts, the man credited with inventing the personal computer, to develop an operating system for Roberts' Altair computer. From those humble beginnings, Gates grew Microsoft into a multi-billion dollar corporation.

The Sierra Nevada is a huge granite mountain range in eastern California. It is more than 400 miles long and covers about 30,000 square miles. When Bill Hewlett was a young boy, he loved to hike and camp in the beautiful mountain ranges of the Sierra Nevada. Even later in life, he remained an avid outdoorsman and took time out from work to ski, mountain climb, and fish.

Chapter 2

A Passion for Science

• •

William Redington Hewlett was born in Ann Arbor, Michigan, on May 20, 1913, but grew up in California. His father, Albion, was a Johns Hopkins–trained doctor and taught medicine at the University of Michigan. The family moved west after Albion Hewlett was invited to join the faculty of Stanford Medical School as a professor, which at that time was located in San Francisco. It was a homecoming for Bill's parents, who had both grown up in San Francisco. And Bill's grandparents had lived in California since the 1800s.

Even as a very young boy, Bill exhibited an almost insatiable curiosity about the world around him and developed an obsessive interest in science. He was particularly fond of electric trains and would spend hours conducting many homemade physics and chemistry experiments. Specifically, he was fascinated with how and why things worked or reacted, although sometimes he would get so wrapped up in his experiments he'd take dangerous risks. One of his regular pastimes was to make explosive powder and blow things up. Years later he would laugh, remembering, "A doorknob is compact—you can put explosives in it, use it as a bomb." However, he also made a point of saying he was very lucky he was never seriously injured, because back in those days, people weren't as educated and aware of safety as they are now.

Looking back as an adult, Hewlett would describe his childhood as "busy and happy." Family vacations were frequently spent outdoors in the Sierra Nevada. These mountains stretch along California's eastern border near Nevada, and back when settlers were coming west in search of gold, the mountains were the last great obstacle on the way to San Francisco.

Hiking and camping in the beautiful mountain ranges of the Sierra Nevada instilled a deep love of nature and the outdoors within Bill. It also spurred his spirit of adventure, which stayed with him long after the vacations were over. Back in San Francisco, Bill would spend hours exploring the rooftops of the city.

Although they were not rich, the Hewlett family lived very comfortably on Albion's salary, and Bill attended a private elementary school. Like many children who grow up in San Francisco, he traveled to and from school on a cable car, enjoying the view of the ocean as the cars clanged up and down the city's many hills.

However, school wasn't nearly as much fun as the ride to get there. Although Bill was a math whiz, able to calculate complicated figures in his head, reading was difficult and frustrating. Except for the fact that he was obviously smart, teachers might have labeled Hewlett as being what was referred to back then as a "slow learner." What nobody knew at the time was that Bill actually suffered from a developmental disorder we would later come to know as dyslexia, which makes it hard to read and write.

Science came easy to Bill, but he struggled in other subjects, such as history and English. Because he didn't understand why he couldn't read the way other kids could, Hewlett found peace and sanctuary in his science lab, which was a place where his learning disability didn't seem to matter.

However, even science classes require learning. Since reading and writing were of such little help to him, Bill developed an amazing ability to listen and memorize what his teachers were saying as they were saying it. He would later describe it as organizing and filing the information he heard in a mental filing cabinet. "This procedure worked particularly well in learning math and science," he would say later to Karen Lewis, the corporate archivist for Hewlett-Packard. Memorization eventually became second nature to Bill, whom Lewis would call "a sponge for information." Years later, after he started his company, employees would marvel at Bill's vast knowledge, with many believing he knew more about more topics than anyone they had ever met.

In school, Bill's reading and writing troubles would soon seem of little importance. When Bill was 12, his father died of a brain tumor. Bill had idolized his father and the loss was devastating to him, as well as to the rest of the family. To try to help Bill and his sister, Louise, overcome their grief, Hewlett's mother and grandmother packed them up and took them to Europe. They ended up in France and would stay for over a year. Although Louise attended a local school, Bill was tutored at home by mother and grandmother, who didn't want his dyslexia to be compounded by his trying to master a new language.

The time spent away with family helped everyone come to grips with Albion's death, and they returned to San Francisco. Bill entered Lowell High School there, which has a place in California history. The school was founded before the Civil War, on August 25, 1856, and produced California's first public high school graduates—seven boys and four girls—three years later, in 1859. Up until then, most schools in California were affiliated with the Catholic missions.

Once again Hewlett was an inconsistent student. In math and science classes, he excelled, impressing students and teachers alike with his grasp of technical subjects. But in his other classes, he was average at best. He found it difficult to muster the concentration necessary to learn in classes that didn't interest him. That inability to focus on less interesting subjects almost cost Bill the opportunity to go to the college he had his heart set on.

From the day it first opened its doors on October 1, 1891, Stanford University was unique. Founded by Leland Stanford and his wife, Jane, the college was intended to be unconventional and nontraditional for its time. For one thing, Stanford was coed, meaning both men and women were accepted, while most universities were male only. Also, the school had no religious affiliation, which was rare in the 1800s.

The Stanfords wanted to create a place of "practical education" that would nurture its students to be both cultured and useful citizens as well as successful in their chosen professions. "I attach great importance to general literature for the enlargement of the mind and for giving business capacity," Leland Stanford said. "I think I have noticed that technically educated boys do not make the most successful businessmen. The imagination needs to be cultivated and developed to assure success in life. A man will never construct anything he cannot conceive."

Such an environment was made for Bill Hewlett. However, first he had to be accepted. But when he asked his high school principal for a recommendation, she was initially reluctant. Looking back at his academic history did not inspire confidence. At best, he was overall just an average student. According to Dave Packard's memoir, *The HP Way,* the troubled principal phoned Bill's mother and said, "Mrs. Hewlett, your son has indicated he wants to go to Stanford. There's nothing in his record to justify my recommending him."

The principal couldn't understand why an apparently disinterested student would want to go to such a challenging university. Mrs. Hewlett explained that Stanford was where Bill's late father had taught. A jolt of recognition struck the principal.

"Was his father Albion Walter Hewlett?" the principal asked, sounding surprised. "He was the best student I ever had." And with that, she wrote Bill a glowing recommendation that got him admitted to Stanford.

Although the principal couldn't imagine it, that recommendation would literally change the course of technology history.

David Packard (left) and William Hewlett (right) met at Stanford University. Because they were both interested in obtaining an electrical engineering degree, they took many of the same classes together. Over time, they became friends and were inspired by a Stanford professor to go into business together. This is an undated Hewlett-Packard Company picture of them.

Chapter 3
The Start of a Beautiful Friendship

• •

Later in his life, Bill Hewlett often told friends that had his father not died, he might have chosen to pursue a career in medicine, mostly to please the parent he so admired. But once in college, he found himself leaning more and more toward electrical engineering. To him, it was an exciting and mentally challenging field of study: it tapped into Bill's desire not only to know how things work, but how to make new gadgets that would work even better.

Bill enrolled at Stanford in 1930. Although he was looking forward to college, it was a difficult time in the country. The stock market crash of 1929 had sent the nation spiraling down into a horrible economic depression that would last right up until America entered World War II. Unemployment skyrocketed, and at its worst 1 out of 3 Americans were out of work. Although the bleak economic outlook for the country might not seem the best time for a would-be inventor, Hewlett refused to be discouraged. He knew how fortunate he and his family were and was thankful to be in the position to go to college. He was determined not to let the black cloud hovering over the country dampen his personal hopes, ambition and ingenuity.

Happily for Bill, his best friend Ed Porter was also attending Stanford. They had grown up together and shared a mutual passion for things electrical. And during his freshman year at Stanford, Bill would meet another kindred spirit, one who would become his lifelong friend and business partner.

David Packard was born in Pueblo, Colorado, in 1912. Although the beautiful cap of Pike's Peak could be seen in the distance, the town of Pueblo was dusty and rough-edged. Its main industry was steel; Pueblo hosted steel mills and foundries that smelted ore from nearby mines.

Like Bill, Dave grew up entertaining himself by playing with explosives—except Packard wasn't so lucky. One day a piece of tubing blew up in his hand, causing permanent damage to his thumb. From that time on, he pursued safer experiments. Like Bill's friend Ed Porter, Dave had a keen interest in radios and once built one from scratch that picked up a station 600 miles away.

In the summer of 1929, between his junior and senior years of high school, Dave and his mother drove to California and visited a friend whose daughter, Alice, had just graduated from Stanford. Alice took Dave on a tour of the campus. Packard was impressed by the school, and he fell in love with its electrical engineering program. He decided that was where he wanted to go to college.

Because they were both interested in pursuing an electrical engineering degree, Packard and Hewlett took many of the same math and science classes and got to know each other. Over time, they became friends, despite having different personalities. People recall Bill as being the less serious of the two. "Hewlett is much more of a lighthearted individual—a bubbly person," Dr. John Linvill, professor emeritus at Stanford, recalled. "He indicated an interest in literally everything. David Packard didn't enjoy life externally as much. But they understood each other's strengths."

Despite their being a bit of an odd couple, Bill and Dave's friendship blossomed. During their junior year in college, they went on an outing and their mutual love of the outdoors brought them even closer. That would be the first of numerous trips they would take together, including a two-week backpack trip in Colorado after their graduation.

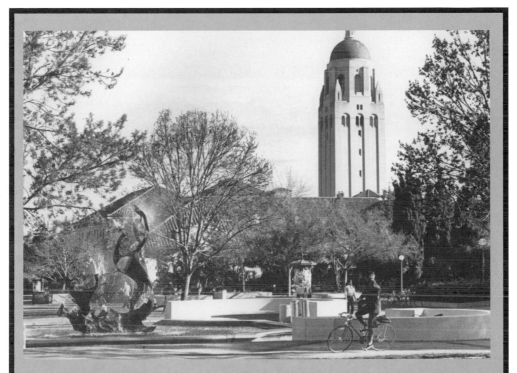

This is a view of White Plaza at Stanford University campus in Stanford, California, taken in 1988. William Hewlett and David Packard both went to school here in the early 1930s.

They were just as compatible in the classroom, even though their specific areas of interest differed. Throughout his years at Stanford, Dave spent a lot of time at the university's amateur radio station, near the engineering section of the campus and the office of a professor named Fred Terman, who would occasionally stop by the radio station and visit. Eventually, Terman suggested that Packard take his graduate course in radio engineering during his senior year. Dave enrolled in the class, intrigued as much by the course as by Terman's reputation.

Fred Terman was already a noted professor when he took Dave Packard under his academic wing. In fact, Terman had practically grown up at Stanford. His father, Lewis, was a famous Stanford psychologist who single-handedly introduced IQ testing in America as part of his groundbreaking research into intelligence and the gifted.

As might be expected, Fred attended Stanford, earning an undergraduate degree in chemistry and a master's degree in electrical engineering. After finishing his Ph.D. at the Massachusetts Institute of Technology (MIT) in 1924, Fred moved back to Stanford, where he began to teach electrical engineering. He would spend his entire career, over 40 years, at Stanford, eventually being named university president. But his greatest legacy is that many of his students would be among the pioneers of Silicon Valley.

It is no accident that Stanford is situated in the heart of Silicon Valley, because Fred Terman would play a pivotal role in the area's technological evolution. In the 1920s and early 1930s, Chicago was the center of the radio industry, and most electrical engineering jobs were there. As Terman's best students graduated, they would head back east for jobs.

It frustrated the professor that so much talent was leaving the West Coast, so he came up with a plan to establish a technology center in the area surrounding Stanford. Terman knew the change from trees to technology wasn't going to happen overnight, but he was patient and began laying the foundation for his plan by handpicking students, such as Dave Packard and Bill Hewlett, for his graduate courses.

Not all Stanford graduates moved back east. Some chose to stay and start their own small companies, hoping to compete with the larger companies of the day, such as Federal Telegraph Company. Part of Terman's curriculum included visits to some of these companies. The professor stressed the very principles Stanford had been founded upon—promoting both imagination and business—in hopes of instilling an entrepreneurial spirit in his students.

Like many of Terman's students, Bill and Dave were inspired by their professor and dreamed of forming their own business. But the financial realities of the Great Depression would force them to put their plan on hold.

David Packard (left) and Bill Hewlett pose in front of the garage in Palo Alto, California where they started the Hewlett-Packard Company. In May of 1989, the garage was dedicated as a state historic landmark as the "birthplace of Silicon Valley."

Chapter 4
An Enduring Influence

● ●

After Hewlett and Packard earned their bachelor of arts degrees in 1934, their original plan was to go into business together—although exactly what kind of business they wanted to pursue had yet to be established. However, when Dave received an unexpected job offer from General Electric, all the way across the country in Schenectady, New York, it forced both young men to reconsider their immediate futures.

In 1934, the United States was still struggling through the Great Depression and good jobs remained scarce. Seeing the devastating effects the Depression had on many neighbors and friends would make a lifelong impression on Bill, who knew how fortunate his family was. He also understood Dave's dilemma, trying to choose between going after his dream or taking a good job. In the end, it was Professor Terman who convinced both his students that taking advantage of the opportunity that had come Dave's way didn't have to mean giving up their hopes of going into business together. Terman encouraged Packard to take the job, believing it would be a good learning experience for any later attempts to start his own business. And while Dave was off working, Terman suggested Bill use the extra time to continue his education and work toward a graduate degree.

So while Packard was studying and absorbing management skills at General Electric, Hewlett kept on studying. Ironically, Bill would also leave California for the

East Coast during this time. After completing his studies at Stanford, Hewlett attended MIT, where he earned his master of science degree in 1936. He immediately returned to Stanford, where he would receive a degree in engineering three years later.

In 1937, Dave Packard came back to Palo Alto to visit his girlfriend, Lucile Salter, and to catch up with Bill. They had their first official business meeting on August 23. They took official notes of everything they talked about, which was mostly about what kind of products they wanted to create and sell. Bill and Dave narrowed it down to manufacturing high-frequency radio receivers and perhaps medical equipment as well. At that meeting, they also discussed what to call the company and thought Engineering Service Company might be good.

The biggest problem, though, was that Dave was still working for General Electric and was nervous about quitting his job if he didn't have any definite prospects. Once again, Professor Terman came to the rescue. He arranged for Packard to get a $500 fellowship that enabled him to move back to California. Likewise, after Bill earned his master's degree, he was offered a job in Chicago. Instead, Professor Terman set him up with a San Francisco doctor who wanted to develop medical equipment, allowing Hewlett the freedom to turn down the job and remain in California. With Dave and Bill settled back in Palo Alto, they were ready to tackle the challenge of starting their long-awaited business.

First, Bill needed to find a place to live that also had enough room to use as a workshop. He rented part of a two-story house on Addison Avenue in Palo Alto. Hewlett moved into a guesthouse on the property, and Dave, who was now married to Lucile (whom everyone called Lu), lived on the ground floor, which had been converted into a separate apartment. The house's garage became their first workshop. Years later, this garage would be named a historical landmark by the state of California as the "birthplace of Silicon Valley." But back in 1938, Bill and Dave were just trying to generate a little income. "We didn't have any plans when we started," Hewlett would later admit. "We were just opportunistic. We did anything to bring in a nickel."

This is the General Electric Building at 30 Rockefeller Center in New York City taken in the latter half of the twentieth century. Dave Packard went to work for GE, though not in this building, when he was a young man just out of Stanford University. Fred Terman at Stanford encouraged Dave to work for GE for a few years, believing that it would be a good learning experience for when he started his own company.

Among their early inventions was a bowling-lane foul indicator for a local bowling alley. The indicator beeped whenever a bowler stepped past the foul line. They also invented a device that automatically flushed a urinal. At the time, Ed Porter was selling air conditioning equipment, and he asked Bill and Dave to design some equipment for his units. They also designed a motor controller that helped the telescope at Lick Observatory track more accurately. But their goal was to find an invention they could mass-produce.

Not surprisingly, it was Fred Terman who got the young partners on the right track. In the spring of 1938, while working in Terman's laboratory, Hewlett developed a resistance-stabilized audio oscillator, a device that produces test tones at specific frequencies for testing either individual sound equipment or entire systems. Terman saw the potential in such a device and set Bill and Dave up with Harold Buttner, who was vice president of research and development for International Telephone and Telegraph. After looking over Bill's oscillator, Buttner offered $500 for the overseas patent rights. He also offered to help them get the invention a United States patent, which gives the inventor exclusive rights so that whoever uses the product has to pay for it. Hewlett and Packard finally had a potentially profitable product to sell.

They built a prototype, or model, of the product by Christmastime 1938. They called their oscillator the 200A, because, said Packard in his autobiography, "We thought it made it sound as if we had been around for a while. We were afraid that if people knew we'd never actually developed, designed and built a finished product before, they'd be scared off."

The price tag for their oscillator was $54.40, which had nothing to do with the actual cost of producing the device. "It reminded us of 54-40 or Fight," explained Packard, which had been the slogan used in 1844 when the U.S. and Canada were establishing the border in the Pacific Northwest. Hewlett and Packard sent out a two-page brochure to 25 prospective customers, most of whom had been suggested by Fred Terman. Then they waited.

On January 1, 1939, Bill and Dave signed an official partnership agreement. They had decided that instead of using Engineering Service Company, they should name it after themselves. To determine whose name should go first, they flipped a coin. Hewlett won and the Hewlett-Packard Company was born. Between them, Bill and Dave put up $528 to start the business, which included the value of a drill press Packard had brought back from New York.

This was the first resistance-stabilized audio oscillator produced by Hewlett-Packard in the 1930s.

Within a few weeks of sending out their brochure, to Bill and Dave's surprise, they had received several orders. So they set to work building the oscillators, cutting the aluminum used for the housing, or outside, of the oscillator in their garage and baking on the paint in Lu's kitchen oven. The housing protected the circuitry inside, which included transmitters and resistors. When finished, the 200A audio oscillator looked like a radio, with a dial on the front and various knobs and switches on the top.

Their biggest break came from Walt Disney Studios. In 1938, Bill had taken the model of the audio oscillator to a technical conference in Portland, Oregon, to get some feedback from other engineers. One of those impressed with the invention was Bud Hawkins, who was the chief sound engineer at Disney. At the time, Hawkins was in the process

Walt Disney, creator of Mickey Mouse, poses at the Pancoast Hotel in Miami, Florida in August 1941. It was the Walt Disney Studios that gave Hewlett-Packard their first big break in business.

of developing sound equipment for a new Disney animated film, *Fantasia*. He had originally planned to buy audio oscillators from a company called General Radio Company for $400 each. But when Bill told Bud he could manufacture his oscillator for under $100, Hawkins eventually decided to take a chance with the newly formed company. In order to meet Hawkins's specific needs, Hewlett had to make some modifications to the original oscillator, resulting in a new model he called the 200B. Disney bought eight of the devices for $71.50 each. It was Hewlett-Packard's first big sale. Not only did it bring in some much-needed cash, it put them on the map as a legitimate company.

At the end of 1939, Hewlett-Packard had earned sales in the amount of $5,369 and made a profit of $1,563. Dave and Bill were finally on their way.

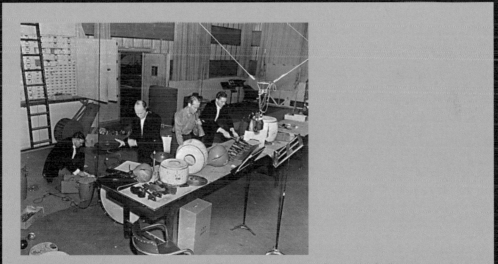

This photo shows the sound effects men at work on Walt Disney's "Fantasia." Bud Hawkins, the chief sound engineer at Disney, decided to take a chance on the newly formed Hewlett-Packard Company and bought their audio oscillators to use in recording the music on eight sound tracks for the revolutionary new film.

The surprise attack on Pearl Harbor on December 7, 1941, forced the United States into World War II. Bill Hewlett was called into active duty and spent the war in the Army Signal Corps, a branch that deals with communications. The company made several products that were used by the U.S. military, and Hewlett-Packard enjoyed huge growth during the war.

Chapter 5
The Spirit of Innovation

• •

Not only was Hewlett's professional life looking up, he had also found personal happiness. In late 1939, Bill married Flora Lamson, a biochemist. He and Flora had known each other since they were children, when their families met on vacation in the Sierras. Hewlett gave up his one-bedroom apartment on Addison Avenue, and the newlyweds moved into a house near Bill and Dave's new shop.

Compared to the garage, the building at the new location seemed huge. It was big enough that the front could be used as an office and the back as their workroom. The only downside was that during rainstorms, water would come flowing down the street and in through the front. Bill and Dave had to put sand bags against the doors to avoid being flooded out.

Making things was second nature to Hewlett and Packard. Since they didn't have Lu's oven anymore to bake the paint onto the cabinets they made, they converted an old refrigerator into an oven, which they kept outside behind the building. However, even scientists and inventors can sometimes make mistakes. They forgot that a refrigerator didn't have the same kind of fireproof insulation an oven would, and one night their oven caught fire. It could have burned the whole building down, but luckily a neighbor saw the flames and called the fire department. Although the converted refrigerator was totaled, there was no damage to the building itself.

With the success of the oscillator under their belts, Bill and Dave's plan was to continue to create instruments that would be used to test and measure sound. Their early products included devices such as a harmonic wave analyzer and several distortion analyzers, which were used to test the clarity of transmitted audio signals. They were convinced that was the right direction to go, even though it meant they would be directly competing with General Radio Company, which at the time was the leading manufacturer of electronic products. General Radio Company is still in business today, although now it is known as GenRad. Products from Hewlett-Packard, which became known as HP, began to win acceptance among engineers and scientists because of their quality. Increased orders meant HP had to grow, and by the end of 1940, Hewlett-Packard had 10 employees.

In the spring of 1941, Bill, who was in the U.S. Army Reserve, was called to active duty. However, the army decided it was more important for Hewlett to continue his work developing electronics, so he was sent back home. Although Hewlett-Packard was not a defense contractor, such as Lockheed Martin, which made airplanes specifically for the Air Force, the electrical components made by Hewlett-Packard were used in the military's communications equipment. After the attack on Pearl Harbor, though, Hewlett was called back to active duty and spent the war in the Army Signal Corps, a group that deals with communications.

Because their products, such as a device that allowed the U.S. Navy to jam the radar of an enemy ship, were used by the military, HP enjoyed huge growth during World War II. By the end of the war, the company was selling over $1 million worth of products a year.

After the war ended in 1945, Hewlett returned to Palo Alto. As they had expected, business slowed down and the number of employees decreased. During that time, Bill and Dave made a conscious effort to expand the company, specifically into the field of microwave test equipment, which was used for tuning audio devices. Microwaves are a type of radio wave. But don't mistake radio waves for sound waves. Radio waves are what travel between a radio station and a radio receiver; sound waves are what come out of the radio after it converts the radio waves to audio.

Bill Hewlett also made an effort to establish the company overseas, foreseeing the potential importance of being an international company. In the spring of 1959, HP opened an office in Geneva, Switzerland, and a production plant in Germany.

The company had grown so much—with more than 300 instruments in their catalog and $30 million in yearly sales—that it was time to reorganize. Bill and Dave formed four groups that would each concentrate on a single family of products: frequency counters, microwave equipment, audio and video products, and oscilloscopes.

But Hewlett never let the business of running a company interfere with his first love, and that was inventing new electronic products. Among the electronics developed by HP were a quartz thermometer that measured temperatures to within .0001 degree Celsius; laser interferometers, which are instruments that use light waves to measure and are accurate up to a millionth of an inch; and LEDs, or light-emitting diodes. These and other inventions would eventually earn *billions* of dollars in revenues for HP.

While Hewlett might have been seen by others as a savvy businessman, at heart he would always be an engineer who loved tinkering in the lab. When he was at the office, Bill would usually have lunch in the company commissary and spend many hours working beside his designers in the HP project labs. He became famous for his belief in his workers. One legendary incident happened when Bill went to get a microscope out of the storeroom one night after regular business hours and discovered the equipment area was locked. He broke off the lock and then wrote a memo to all the HP managers. The memo read: "Hewlett-Packard trusts its employees" and insisted the equipment lockers always be left open so that his designers would have the freedom, day or night, to work on their projects should an inspiration hit them.

Bill Hewlett (left) visits Dave at The Hewlett Packard Company during the war.

The HP-35, the world's first scientific handheld calculator.

It was his belief that giving his employees as creative an environment as possible is what allowed the company to develop so many products. In 1972, HP developed a product that was truly revolutionary: the first handheld scientific calculator. For the first time in history, it was possible to make complicated calculations, including trigonometry, instantaneously with more accuracy than a slide rule. And it fit into a shirt pocket.

The calculator had been Hewlett's brain child. Under Bill's direction, one of HP's engineers put together some drawings of what Bill had in mind and then forwarded the sketches to an industrial design group. About a month later, the first plastic prototype was built. It was called the HP-35 because it had 35 keys. When the calculator was shipped to stores, it created a sensation, because now it was possible for anyone to solve everyday problems, such as computing interest rates, quickly and accurately. Over 100,000 of the calculators sold the first year alone. NASA had astronauts use an HP handheld calculator aboard their spacecraft in order to calculate the exact angle to reenter Earth's atmosphere. So common are handheld calculators now that it is hard to imagine the impact this product had when it first came out, but it is considered to be a product that truly changed the world.

Typically, Hewlett was not content to let himself or his company rest on past achievements. So he turned his attention to what he believed was the next great technological breakthrough—the personal computer.

Steve Wozniak went to work for Hewlett Packard in 1973. He spent all his time working with electronics chips for calculators. In his spare time, using H-P equipment, Woz created a circuit board designed to run a new, relatively inexpensive microprocessor for a computer. He offered the design to Hewlett-Packard, but no one there was interested in making personal computers. So, H-P released its interest in the circuit boards and Wozniak and Steve Jobs formed Apple Computer Company.

Chapter 6

The HP Way

· ·

Even though Bill Hewlett was still very active in the company, by the early 1970s he started preparing for the time he and Dave would finally turn over the day-to-day control of the company to others. The direction the company would take was clearly set in motion in 1972 when HP expanded into the computer business.

Ironically, perhaps the biggest business mistake Bill Hewlett ever made was over computers. Steve Wozniak, an engineer at HP, presented his idea of a "personal" computer to his bosses. At the time, Bill didn't think HP was well positioned enough to expand in that direction. In his autobiography, Dave Packard recalled his partner saying, "Don't try to take a fortified hill, especially if the army on top is bigger than your own."

When HP chose not to pursue the personal computer concept, Wozniak quit his job and in 1976 teamed with Steve Jobs to start Apple Computer. In another bit of irony, they too started their company in an old garage. However, what many people don't realize is that today, HP actually sells more computers than Apple and is now the second-largest computer company in the world. That's because even though Bill Hewlett hadn't wanted to pursue the personal computer, he did realize the importance of computers in improving the quality of the company's electronic instruments: computers could make them faster and more powerful. He set about taking advantage of that potential.

In 1972, the same year the handheld calculator was released, HP introduced its first general-purpose business computer, the HP3000, which was used primarily for data processing for high-technology engineering and research. The HP line of computers was a huge success, but the company's greatest legacy was its work with printers.

Although Bill was retired from running the company on a daily basis, his vision continued to drive the company forward. With the personal computer boom of the 1980s, he and Dave saw a new opportunity to invent an inexpensive, convenient printer. At the time, most printers were "impact printers," which worked more like a typewriter, with a mechanical part actually striking the paper. Dot matrix and daisy wheel printers were the most common. But Bill believed the future of printers would be in what was called nonimpact printing, such as laser printers, which work by using pulses of light, or ink-jet printers, which use electrically charged ink that is conformed into letters. Ink-jet printers use extremely small droplets of ink—smaller than the diameter of a human hair. A series of nozzles spray the drops of ink directly on the paper.

Although HP had introduced the first industrial laser printer in 1982, it was extremely expensive, costing $100,000, and was the size of a refrigerator. Just two years later the company introduced the first HP LaserJet, which sold for $3,495. The LaserJet II had what was then a revolutionary feature—the ability to print in the correct order. Up until then a document being printed off a computer could only start with the first page and end with the last, meaning the pages were always out of proper order. The laser would print "back to front" so that the document you picked up was in proper sequence. The HP DeskJet was just as revolutionary because it introduced color printing and, because it was so affordable, is credited for finishing off the dot matrix printer industry. Dot matrix printers were much slower, the quality of the print looked inferior to that of a laser or ink-jet printer, and they lacked the capacity to print in color. And while impact printers used inked ribbon, the laser printer had a self-contained replaceable toner cartridge, so it was neater to maintain.

When Hewlett would look back at all that he, Dave and their company had accomplished, he would always give credit to his employees. Others, however, would credit Bill and Dave's revolutionary management style as what truly fostered the ingenuity and creativity of their workers.

Bill did everything he could to encourage innovation. He felt the best way to accomplish this was to create a comfortable work environment. It was his firm belief that everyone wants to do a good job, and he developed what was called "management by walking about." Whenever he was at the office, he would spend the day walking around, talking and interacting with the engineers. He let them know what the company's goals were and then gave them a lot of flexibility to achieve those goals in their own individual way.

Dave and Bill's management style had been greatly influenced by the way their old professor, Fred Terman, had treated his students and run his laboratory. If it worked at Stanford, why wouldn't it work at a business? So when Hewlett and Packard started out, they agreed to run their company very differently from the way companies were run back then. They committed to help their employees, both creatively and financially: the work areas were open, and employees could walk into their bosses' offices at any time to pitch ideas. They gave their managers a lot of responsibility in making decisions. They frequently helped out competitors, believing it would ultimately be good for everyone to work together to solve problems. They provided catastrophic medical insurance (which protected workers in case of serious illness), had everyone call each other by their first names and regularly hosted employee parties and picnics, where they would cook and serve the food. In addition, they made a commitment to be both good citizens and to give back to the university that had given them their start.

The business philosophy started by Dave and Bill became known as the HP Way. It has become a model for businesses around the world. In the early years, Flora Hewlett would give a blanket to any employee who had a baby. Years later, all employees were given shares of stock so that they could share in the company's success.

Bill and Dave worked together to build one of the most successful electronics companies of the twentieth century.

As Dave Packard noted, "You've got to have leadership, you've got to know what you're doing, and you've got to play it straight." Bill added, "You've got to have concern for what your people do. We felt this work force should be able to share to some extent in the progress of the company. We did not want to run a hire-and-fire operation, but rather a company based on a loyal and dedicated work force. "

For as savvy a businessman as Hewlett was, he was an even greater philanthropist. Over the years, HP donated more than $300 million to Stanford University, as well as $25 million for the establishment of a Frederick Terman Fellowship to honor the Stanford professor who was their mentor and inspiration.

Hewlett was also committed to environmental causes, donating millions to ecology efforts and to preserving California's Lake Tahoe and Sierra regions.

Hewlett worked almost daily until 1993. In the last years of his life, he was slowed by a number of strokes. Although his body was fragile, his mind remained nimble and sharp. He lived long enough to see more than 30,000 electronic, computer, and software companies call Silicon Valley their home and has been revered as one of the area's most influential founding fathers.

William Hewlett died January 12, 2001. In a National Public Radio interview, Karen Lewis, HP's historian, remembered him as "very, very friendly, warm, twinkly; incredibly bright. He had a mischievous glint in his eye, and there wasn't a time that I didn't see Mr. Hewlett when he didn't ask me a question that was a challenge. He leaves a tremendous legacy in Silicon Valley, and Silicon Valley has made a tremendous mark on the world."

William Hewlett Chronology

1913 Born in Ann Arbor, Michigan

1916 Father is hired as a professor at Stanford and family moves to California

1925 Father dies of brain tumor

1930 Enters Stanford, where he strikes up a friendship with Dave Packard

1936 Earns master's degree in electrical engineering from Massachusetts Institute of Technology

1938 Bill and Dave establish their first workshop on Addison Avenue; Bill designs audio oscillator in Fred Terman's lab

1939 Forms the Hewlett-Packard company with Dave; earns engineering degree from Stanford; marries Flora Lamson

1941 to 1945 Serves as an officer in the Army Signal Corps

1954 Elected President of the Institute of Electrical and Electronics Engineers

1950s Implements groundbreaking working conditions and employee benefits

1957 Begins building HP corporate building in Palo Alto

1958 Appointed Director of Stanford Medical Center

1959 Opens HP office in Switzerland and plant in Germany

1966 Establishes the William and Flora Hewlett Foundation; President Lyndon B. Johnson appoints Hewlett to the Science Advisory Committee Early

1970s Develops idea for handheld scientific calculator

1972 HP expands into computer business

1977 Flora Hewlett dies

1978 Marries Rosemary Bradford; retires as HP Chief Executive Officer but remains active in the company

1983 Awarded National Medal of Science, the nation's highest scientific honor

1996 Dave Packard dies

2001 Dies on January 12

Computer Timeline

3000 B.C.   Dust abacus is invented, probably in Babylonia.

1622 A.D.   William Oughtred develops the slide rule in England.

1623   Wilhelm Schickard designs the first mechanical calculator, for astronomers.

1673   Gottfried Leibniz builds a mechanical calculating machine that multiplies, divides, adds and subtracts.

1886   Heinrich Hertz produces and detects electromagnetic, or radio, waves; William Burroughs develops the first commercially successful mechanical adding machine.

1901   Reception of transatlantic radio signals in Newfoundland from Guglielmo Marconi in the U.K.

1904   Sir John Ambrose Fleming invents the vacuum tube and diode.

1907   Lee de Forest patents the Audion.

1938   Hewlett-Packard Co. is founded to make electronic equipment.

1940   First color TV broadcast.

1947   John Bardeen, Walter Brattain, and William Shockley of Bell Telephone Laboratories invent the transistor.

1958   At Texas Instruments, Jack Kilby builds the first integrated circuit.

1958   Robert Noyce develops a miniaturized integrated circuit that can be reliably manufactured.

1968   Robert Noyce cofounds Intel (Integrated Electronics).

1972   Hewlett-Packard introduces first pocket calculator, making slide rules obsolete overnight; Bill Gates and Paul Allen form Traf-O-Data, which was renamed Microsoft three years later

1976   Apple Computer is born

1984   Apple introduces the MacIntosh Computer, the first computer to effectively manipulate graphics

1982   Hewlett-Packard adopts the three-inch floppy disk for general use.

1988   Hewlett-Packard introduces the DeskJet inkjet printer.

1990   Apple Computer's AppleLink is renamed America Online

2002   H-P and Compaq merge into one company

Further Reading

Cohen, Judith Love, and David A. Katz (illustrator). *You Can Be a Woman Engineer* (Culver City, Calif.: Cascade Pass, 2000).

Gaines, Ann. *Steve Jobs* (Bear, Delaware: Mitchell Lane, 2001).

Packard, David. *The HP Way: How Bill Hewlett and I Built Our Company* (New York: HarperCollins, 1995).

Riddle, John, and Jim Whiting. *Stephen Wozniak and the Story of Apple Computer* (Bear, Delaware: Mitchell Lane, 2002).

Internet Addresses

"A Chronology of Computer History"
http://www.cyberstreet.com/hcs/museum/chron.htm
"The History of Hewlett-Packard"
http://www.hp.com/hpinfo/abouthp/histnfacts/
"Lee de Forest," Biography
http://chem.ch.huji.ac.il/~eugeniik/history/deforest.htm
Tajnai, Carolyn E. "Fred Terman, The Father of Silicon Valley"
http://www.netvalley.com/archives/mirrors/terman.html

Glossary

amplifier: A device that takes in a weak electric signal and sends out a stronger one.

Audion: A special kind of vacuum tube that can be used to amplify weak electric signals. The Audion was used in the Bell Telephone system, as well as in early radios and computers. It was eventually replaced in most applications by the transistor.

audio oscillator: A device that produces test tones at specific frequencies for testing sound equipment.

diode: Also called a rectifier; an electronic device with two wires or terminals that allows electric current to flow through in only one direction and is used for converting alternating current into direct current. Rectifiers were important for use in radios, which required direct current to power the amplifiers that drove speakers or headphones.

electric signal: Information expressed through changes in an electric current. Sound waves, for example, can be converted to electricity by a microphone and sent as an electric signal through the wires of a stereo to the speakers.

electrode: An electrical lead or wire attached to any electronic device or circuit through which current may flow in or out.

element: Any of over a hundred fundamental materials containing only one kind of atom. Some common elements are oxygen, gold, hydrogen, and silicon. All other materials are made of compounds or mixtures of elements. Water, for example, is made of two hydrogen atoms attached to one oxygen atom.

entrepreneur: A person who assumes the financial risk of beginning and managing a new business.

fellowship: Money awarded for education sponsored by an organization or institution such as a college.

frequency counter: An electronic instrument or circuit that displays the frequency of an incoming signal.

integrated circuit: A collection of transistors and electrical circuits all built onto a single crystal usually made of silicon. Also called a computer chip.

LED (light-emitting diode): A diode that produces either visible or infrared light as a by-product of electricity passing through it. LEDs require very little power and are often used as indicator lights on computers.

oscillator: A device for producing alternating current; a radio-frequency or audio-frequency generator.

oscilloscope: A device that draws a graph of an electrical signal. In most applications the graph shows how signals change over time: the vertical (Y) axis represents voltage and the horizontal (X) axis represents time.

patent: A document issued by a national government granting an inventor exclusive rights to an invention for a limited time.

radio receiver: A device for converting radio waves into sounds.

resistance: The amount a substance resists or restricts the flow of electric current. Devices with a specific resistance, called resistors, are used in electronic circuits.

semiconductor: A solid crystalline substance that can conduct electricity well but not as well as a conductor such as copper wire. Some common semiconductors are silicon and germanium. Transistors are made out of semiconductor crystals.

silicon: A nonmetallic element used to make electronic circuits.

transistor: Short for "transfer resistance." Transistors are tiny devices that can be control the flow of electricity. They can amplify an electrical signal, or they can switch on and off, letting current through or blocking it as necessary.

vacuum tube: A device consisting of a number of electrodes contained within an otherwise empty enclosure.

Index